ASSHOLE HAIKU

ASSHOLE HAIKU

'Celebrating' The Assholes in Our Everyday Lives

James Weir

ISBN 978-1-7772280-3-3

Dedicated to

Leslie, Annie and Sultan

They're not assholes

Foreword

Asshole [as-ˌ(h)ōl]

"usually vulgar: a stupid, annoying, or detestable person"

Ierriam Webster, 2020. Asshole. Retrieved from tps://www.merriam-webster.com/dictionary/asshole)

The asshole. They're everywhere. You can't void them. From sun-up to sun-down, you're kely going to encounter at least one during your ay. What can you do about it? Why nothing, of ourse.

In that light, join us as we dissect the asshole, :elebrate' their existence, and, hopefully, exact a ttle mental revenge on their being.

Do they even know?
Assholes are not self-aware
Ignorance is bliss

Parking lot door ding
No apology note left
I hope you get keyed

Nostrils flare at stench
Fart left in elevator
Asshole vapor trail

The sidewalk gawkers
Strolling in everyone's way
Please walk into road

Thank you for sharing
Your mix-tape of death metal
From your apartment

Please rev your engine
At the crack of six a.m.
Who needs alarm clock?

Toilet paper gone
Empty roll just hanging there
How to wipe my ass

Handicap parking
Asshole doesn't look or care
Please become crippled

Cell phone on the bus
Screaming so all can hear you
Fuck you for sharing

Cyclists are special
Rules of the road don't apply
Please get broad-sided

Eight items or less
It's posted there on the sign
Cannot read OR count

Giant souped-up truck
Beautiful, powerful
Shame about small dick

Pandemic assholes
No social distance or mask
They're deadly assholes

Bad body odor
Gagging me on the subway
Please sit in next car

Teen-age behavior
Talking back, not listening
Face it – they're assholes

Screaming neighbor's kids
Parents don't care about noise
Assholes start somewhere

Took two parking spots
“My ride deserves protection”
Again, small penis

Surfers as assholes? Apparently they can be Cowabunga Rude!

Julian Assange
Strikes me as quite the asshole
Probably smells too

Am I an asshole?
If you think to ask yourself
Then the answer's no

Cyclists ignore signs
Why do I keep dissing them?
Because they're assholes

You know what they say
Write regarding what you know
Getting concerned now

The shared office fridge
Garlic sandwich stinks it up
What asshole brought that?

Behold "Manspreading"
Asshole mating ritual
Working for you much?

Brutal labor pains
"Just breathe and push harder, dear"
Men are all assholes

Milk carton empty
Why did you put it back in?
Hidden cow in there?

Is Trump an asshole?
It seems rather obvious
In fact, he's their King

Cyclists don't obey
Barreling through the stop sign
Sorry I ran you down

Tantrums by toddlers
Smashing the other kids' toys
It starts young for some

The high school bully
Made life hell for all those years
Hope you’re fat and bald

Pedophile clergy
Wrong interest in assholes
Can't make this funny

The lazy asshole
Familiar to all wives
The couch is his lair

I can't stop thinking
About the assholes in my life
Ulcer getting worse…

Take second-hand smoke
Smokers infringe on your health
Cancer waits for them

Neighbor smoking weed
Smells like a dead skunk's asshole
And so does the weed

Think about Shakespeare
The bane of your English class
He deserves mention

King Henry the Eighth
A bad wife? Off with her head!
A Royal Asshole

What makes an asshole?
Psychologically broken?
No refunds sadly

Prick, bitch or asshole
A spectrum of bad-actors
No contrast really

Religious zealots
Assholes in the name of God
God is not happy

How about your ex?
A definite you-know-what
Goes without saying

All the Flat Earthers
Denying the obvious
The label does fit

High school gym teacher
Eligible to add to
The expanding list

The post-game riot
Assholes travel in large packs
Hope your moms are proud

Not sure if you're one?
If you've never thought of it
You are an asshole

"It's not a problem"
The climate change deniers
Yep – you're in the club

All impaired drivers
“I’m O.K. – give me my keys”
You’re beyond asshole

"The glass is half-full!"
Motivational speakers
Paid to be assholes

About bad bosses
Where do they all arise from?
Selected at birth

They say in business
“Customer is always right”
Not if they’re assholes

Asshole genesis?
Genetics? Environment?
Bit of both I think

Dogs are not assholes
Cats are different story
Sorry, but it's true

Frustrating commute
One slow car in the fast lane
One guess who's driving

Nation of assholes?
No one thinks it's <u>their</u> country
We're not naming names

The jerks at Starbucks
With twelve-syllable orders
Just get a coffee

You know the saying
"Opinions are like assholes
We have all got one"

Science deniers
Evolution is a sham
You seem to prove it

The Murder Hornets
Assholes of the insect world
Seems no group's immune

Took the last donut
Without asking anyone first
Hope you choke on it

What was I thinking?
A Liberal Arts degree?
I'm the asshole here

Hipsters in Blundstones
Sitting in Starbucks writing
It's their own club house

Ambulance blaring
The asshole won't pull over
Hope you need one soon

Take the word "asshole"
It has a nice ring to it
(No pun intended)

Long fast-food lineup
They can’t decide what they want
You know what you are

They come in all types
Dyslexic assholes exist
All Assholes Untie!

The drive-thru asshole
Blaring your stereo loud
Hope your order's wrong

Women as assholes?
I have no doubt they can be
Wife says I'm wrong though…

All stuck-up celebs
Think they're all better than us
They're not – just assholes

Nurses as assholes?
Certainly, but don't let on
Needles really hurt

Bad motorcyclist
Racing like a fool on road
Donate your organs

Describing assholes
Narcissist. Sociopath.
All of those and more

Is Mark Zuckerberg
Part of the asshole union?
Nah. Just autistic

Asshole stimulant?
Way too much booze comes to mind
Need more happy drunks

Think of The Simpsons
Mr. Burns. Mayor Quimby
BIG cartoon assholes

Warning to assholes
Don’t piss off the café staff
Spit not good to eat

Office co-worker
Making cubicle life hell
Shut the fuck up please

All-female workplace
Crashing waves of estrogen
Not assholes (see wife)

Dennis Leary sings
You-tube his great song 'Asshole'
Still holds up today

Drunken partier
Dropping a deuce on my lawn
Eat shit (yours) and die

Library talkers
Can’t study for my exams
Hope you bomb the test

The "Porch Pirates"
Do I even need to add
Your kind to the list?

Jerk at the Doctor's
Makes waiting room horrible
Hope prostate check hurts

Assholes for assholes
Display your "Brown Ring of Shame"
A medal for your class

"I guess I was wrong"
Said no real asshole ever
A sad fact of life

Harvey Weinstein jailed
Asshole's asshole is sore now
Karma is a bitch

Asshole prowls the bar
Won't take no for an answer
Sucks to be a girl

Coronavirus
Now there's a major asshole
Please just go away

Need reader input
[insert your nemesis here]
Yes, they're an asshole

Trump's a hero in
The annals of assholedom
Yes, there's a pun there

Think of Roseanne Barr
Was a racist, blamed her meds
It was NOT the meds…

The good die too soon
But assholes live on and on
Certainly not fair

The sports-moms and -dads
"Play my son 'cause he's the best"
Please go bench yourselves

When assholes argue
'Tis a clash of the titans
Only one will live

Paranoid asshole
Conspiracy everywhere
Tin foil hats for all

Arsehole, asshat, prick
Jackass, dickhead, idiot
All still an asshole

Think introspection
Try to learn from your mistakes
Let <u>us</u> enjoy peace

Barge into the line
Just like you're God's chosen one
News flash – God hates you

Bogus faith healers
Preying on the faithful sheep
Yep. You're one. No doubt

Racist policeman
'Driving while black' is a crime?
You're the criminal

Immigrant bashers
"They take all our jobs" seems weird
<u>You</u> won't take those jobs

Take testosterone
The hormone of the asshole
Neutering might help

Thank you for reading
Supporting all my writing
You're not an asshole

Also by James Weir:

Coronavirus Haiku – Poetry to Help Lighten Your Pandemic Days

About the Author

When he's not busy being a poet (and we use the term poet very loosely here), James Weir is a small animal veterinarian. In addition to clinical practice, he holds graduate degrees in pathology and in public health. He has also worked as a stand-up comedian. He has been published before, but mostly boring science crap. This is his second book of poetry (again, we use this term very loosely).

www.ingramcontent.com/pod-product-compliance
Lightning Source LLC
Chambersburg PA
CBHW031350060726
47590CB00007B/2719

* 9 7 8 1 7 7 7 2 2 8 0 3 3 *